Empath:

The Most Effective Empath Healing and Empath Survival Guide in Today's World for Highly Sensitive People to Protect Yourself and Enjoy Life. Empath Rising!

Table of Contents

Introduction

Chapter One: What Does It Mean to Be an Empath?.....14

    Scientific Theories

    Characteristics of an Empath

    The Making of an Empath

Chapter Two: Understanding an Empath.....28

    Empathy vs. Empaths

    Measuring the Sensitivity of Empaths

    Types of Empaths

    How Empaths Interact with Others

    Advantages of Being an Empath

    Disadvantages of Being an Empath

Chapter Three: How to Have Healthy Relationships.....45

Challenges That Empaths Face in Intimate Relationships

Why Empaths Make the Best Partners

Reasons to Be in a Relationship with an Empath

Dealing with Family and Friends

Empaths and Narcissists

Relationship Advice for Empaths

Chapter Four: How to Be a Parent as an Empath.....63

Parenting

Nurturing Empathic Children

How to Know If Your Child Is an Empath?

Chapter Five: How to Thrive in the World of Work as an Empath.....77

A Changing Work Environment

Understanding Energy

Creating Boundaries

Choosing Careers

The Best Jobs for Empaths

Healthcare

The Worst Jobs for Empaths

Chapter Six: Why Some Empaths Turn to Addiction.....98

Medication and Empaths

Chapter Seven: How to Protect Yourself as an Empath......105

Energy Fields

Taking Care of Yourself

Healthy Living

Exercise

Meditation

Good Judgment

Listening to Your Instincts

Spiritual Guidance

Breathing

A Time Out

Some Tips on How to Keep Centered

Tips to Renounce Toxic Energy

Chapter Eight: The Benefits of Meditation.....128

Medical Benefits

The Basics

Effective Release

Types of Meditation

   Metta Meditation

   Body Scan or Progressive Relaxation

   Mindfulness Meditation

   Breath Awareness Meditation

- Kundalini Yoga
- Zen Meditation
- Transcendental Meditation

Tips for Successful Meditation:

Mindfulness

- Yoga
- Breathing from the Abdomen
- Breathing from the Nostrils

Chapter Nine: How Empaths Have Helped the World.....150

- Empaths in Politics
- Empathic Actors
- Empathy Through Authors
- Social Activists

Conclusion.....158

© Copyright 2018 by Judith Guise - All rights reserved.

The follow eBook is reproduced below with the goal of providing information that is as accurate and reliable as possible. Regardless, purchasing this eBook can be seen as consent to the fact that both the publisher and the author of this book are in no way experts on the topics discussed within and that any recommendations or suggestions that are made herein are for entertainment purposes only. Professionals should be consulted as needed prior to undertaking any of the action endorsed herein.

This declaration is deemed fair and valid by both the American Bar Association and the Committee of Publishers Association and is legally binding throughout the United States.

Furthermore, the transmission, duplication or reproduction of any of the following work including specific information will be considered an illegal act irrespective of if it is done electronically or in print. This extends to creating a secondary or tertiary copy of the work or a recorded copy and is only allowed with express written consent from the Publisher. All additional right reserved.

The information in the following pages is broadly considered to be a truthful and accurate account of facts and as such any inattention, use or misuse of the information in question by the reader will render any resulting actions solely under their purview. There are no scenarios in which the publisher or the original author of this work can be in any fashion deemed liable for any hardship or damages that may befall them after undertaking information described herein.

Additionally, the information in the following pages is intended only for informational purposes and should thus be thought of as universal. As befitting its nature, it is presented without assurance regarding its prolonged validity or interim quality. Trademarks that are mentioned are done without written consent and can in no way be considered an endorsement from the trademark holder.

Introduction

In a high-stimulus world, many people struggle with the onslaught of input in various forms. Our senses are bombarded, and if limits are not set, this bombardment and sensory overload can be continuous. Research has shown that our autonomous nervous systems are becoming extra sensitive because of this overload. This leads to all kinds of ailments like hormone imbalances and compromised immune systems. Empaths have to deal with this in an exponentially greater way. They are wired to feel things so much more deeply and passionately. Empaths not only feel all these emotions but absorb and take on the energies of people that they are surrounded with. The more people, the more chaos, the more they absorb the turmoil and negativity.

Empaths rely on their feelings and intuition as the filter through which they interact with the world. They are giving, compassionate, excellent friends, but one of the most attractive qualities of empaths is their ability to completely understand you and to truly listen. This can leave empaths open and vulnerable to abuse by others, emotional exhaustion and the need for isolation. This often leaves them misunderstood by others, relegating them to a world of seclusion or addiction.

This book explores what it is to be an empath. It explores the ideas around what, and more importantly, why they are experiencing what they do. Empaths and people surrounded by empaths can better understand their behaviors and responses in situations and can be better equipped to help them if necessary or be a support structure for them. Many empaths can result in depressions, social anxiety, panic attacks or a range of addictions if they do not understand what is happening to them and how to protect themselves. This book will teach you that empaths do not need to feel overwhelmed all the time. By recognition, understanding, and acceptance, one can navigate the world successfully. It is also meant to inspire empaths to embrace their purpose in life by looking at how some famous empaths changed the world. This book provides techniques and tools to live a fuller, happier life as an empath.

This book is to validate and affirm empaths who may be feeling confused and overwhelmed. Whether you are, or someone you know is an empath, this will help you gain a better understanding and appreciation of what it means to be an empath in the modern world. This is extremely important as it can change our world.

Chapter One: What Does It Mean to Be an Empath?

Who is an empath? Have you found that you become extremely emotional around pain, cruelty, and loss, to the point where you will not watch certain movies, the news, or you find yourself staying away from social media? Do you find that this emotion can stay with you for days and that it can be difficult to shake off? Perhaps you were always told that you were too sensitive as a child. Sometimes you feel misunderstood by people thinking you are avoiding relevant and topical issues, and you should rather be pro-active in trying to solve them. People do not understand that the emotion you feel can be crippling. If any of this feels familiar to you, you may well be an empath.

Living in a world filled with injustice, pain, and suffering can be very daunting for an empath. As you might have guessed, the word empath comes from 'empathy'. The dictionary defines empathy as the ability to relate, understand, and share the feelings of someone else. Empaths do this, but it is on an exponentially deeper level. Empaths, therefore absorb the energies of the world, this can be negative ones associated with stress and pain or positive ones associated with joy and love. Experiencing these emotions to such an extreme level can make one feel slightly lost and misunderstood by others. You can feel like you just don't belong. However, being an empath can be one of the greatest skills you can have if you learn how to live with it.

Empaths are people who are extremely susceptible to the emotions of others. This ability to relate so personally to others makes empaths one of the best nurturers, listeners, and givers that you will find. Empaths compassion for people can leave them feeling exhausted, but the good news is that they can develop strategies to create boundaries and protect their feelings.

Scientific Theories

For those skeptics who think empaths belong to the category of fairies and folktales, there are five interesting scientific arguments for empaths and empathy.

Electromagnetic Fields

The heart and brain both create electromagnetic fields which transmit information about people's feelings and thoughts. Empaths are incredibly sensitive to these fields. These fields can be documented and provide scientific evidence of what empaths engage with.

__Mirror Neuron System__

It has been discovered that there are cells in the brain that mirror people's emotions. When your child is hurt at school, you feel hurt too. When your spouse gets an increase, you feel their joy as well. Empaths are thought to have hyper-sensitive mirror neurons compared to other people and therefore can relate to and feel deep compassion for others—even strangers. Conversely, "*empathy deficient disorders*" like sociopaths, psychopaths, narcissists, and even people with autism have desensitized mirror neurons and do not feel empathy toward others. Experiments have been done and measured through fMRI, which are basically scans of the brain activity. These scans show how closely scans of empaths and candidates match each other.

Emotional Contagion

Have you ever wondered why when one baby starts to cry, it sets off other babies around it? Or when you yawn you make people around you yawn? It is more common than you think for people to take on other people's emotions. This phenomenon is called emotional contagion. Research has even shown that this ability to synchronize feelings is important for relationships. Empaths experience this at a deeper level than most people.

Synesthesia

Synesthesia is when a person experiences

more than one sense simultaneously. For example, a person could see colors when they listen to music. Isaac Newton is a well-known synesthetic. "*Mirror-touch synesthesia*" is a neurological condition where some rare individuals can actually experience similar sensations or emotions of others as if it were their own. For example, these people could feel an abdominal pain that they observe in another. Many empaths will relate to the "*Mirror-touch synesthesia*" condition.

Dopamine

Dopamine is a neurotransmitter that is linked with the pleasure response. There are many studies that have shown that dopamine affects the empathic perceptions and responses in people. People with a high sensitivity to dopamine need less dopamine to experience joy. They can take pleasure from simple activities like reading and walking in nature rather than high stimulation from parties etc. People with a low sensitivity to dopamine need to have to do a lot more to experience joy. Therefore it is understandable why empaths will readily feel the joy of others.

Empaths and Highly Sensitive People

Empaths are often confused with highly sensitive people. Highly sensitive people do not need much stimulation. They may experience sensitivity to the senses or avoid people and large crowds. They have things in common with empaths like alone time, helping others and a passion for nature. But empaths take these experiences to a higher level. They can sense and absorb the energy of others, sometimes to the extent that they can't distinguish it from their own emotions. Highly sensitive people and empaths are not mutually exclusive; there are many people who are both.

Characteristics of an Empath

If you have been able to identify with many of the traits already discussed, you may well be an empath or know of one. Here are a few more characteristics that may help you recognize the traits.

Empaths are Great Listeners
Because they can identify with what you are saying. They make amazing friends because they can relate to what you are feeling and will do whatever they can to help.

They are Nurturers and Caregivers
Whether good or bad, negative or positive, empaths will absorb these energies. If they take on more negative energies, they will feel exhausted; if they are surrounded by positive energies, they will thrive.

Empaths Do Not Cope Well in Crowds

They prefer to either be alone or have smaller social groups. This is a natural consequence of absorbing the energies around them. In crowds, this energy absorption is increased tenfold. The avoidance of crowds and large groups of people make empaths introverted people.

Empaths use their intuition

They use intuition to engage with the world, and therefore, have a highly developed sense of intuition. They need to take time to stop and recognize what they are feeling before it has any negative implications for them.

Alone Time Is Super Important for Empaths

It is the time they use to recharge and re-energize. This need for alone time often makes empaths shy away from intimate relationships. There may be an underlying fear that they absorb too much of the other person and lose themselves. There are some people that drain your energy or peace of mind. An empath is particularly vulnerable to these energy zappers, as they are drawn from the emotional sensitivity of empaths and can eventually affect them negatively.

Everything Natural Replenishes, Revives and Restores an Empath

They take refuge in nature and seek out time in the wilderness. Empaths have highly sensitized senses and cannot cope with excessive noise, talking and smells. Empaths love to help people, but this leads to them taking on those energies to their own detriment.

Remember, being able to recognize if you are or anyone you know is an empath, is the first step. These established steps and guidelines can be followed to protect yourself and create balance.

The Making of an Empath

So what makes people become empaths? Is it nature? Or nurture? There are a number of reasons why people develop or intensify their sensitivities.

Nature
Many mothers will notice that their newborns are more sensitive to touch, smell, movement, sound, light, and temperature when they are born. This would suggest an inherent inclination towards being an

empath. Sometimes empaths pass on these characteristics genetically to their offspring.

Nurture

The trauma suffered as a child may lead to increased sensitivity levels as an adult. These children may feel a greater sense of not being valued or heard as the trauma wears down their defenses. They may feel increasingly helpless as they take on negative emotions of those around them. Conversely, a supportive environment can see an empath child thrive into a healthy and powerful adult.

Whichever the cause, the symptoms are the same: crowds, bright lights, noise, an angry person—can all lead to a sensory overload for an empath. The important point to remember is that there is a way forward, and we address all the things you can do as an empath, no matter what your background—to understand, heal, and protect yourself. Empaths, unlike other people, need to learn to defend themselves against stress, they are different. A noxious stimulus, such as an angry person, crowds, noise, or bright lights can agitate us since our threshold for sensory overload is extremely low.

Chapter Two:
Understanding an Empath

In a world that may often seem like it has gone insane, where we have reached cruelty of immense heights in the name of religion and justice; where there have been far too many genocides to mention, and with slavery in all its forms still existing—empathy is a quality that is seriously lacking. It is the human quality that can solve the cruelties of the world. It enables us to have compassion and respect for one another. It opens our hearts to others and encourages acceptance and understanding of others. It is our pathway towards peace, and therefore becomes vitally important that we recognize it, value it and learn how to best use this gift.

To do this, we need to take a deeper understanding of what it means to be an empath.

Empathy vs. Empaths

The first step in doing that is to distinguish empathy from empaths. As stated before empathy is the ability to relate to, understand and share the feelings of someone else. Basically, you can empathize with someone going through a rough time, or you can be genuinely happy for someone who has just achieved something. Empaths can feel these emotions more purely and genuinely. It affects them on a much deeper and real level. There is no filter whether it is joy or sadness. Empaths feel things before they think—which is different from how the rest of society operates. It may be a little difficult to process because we are a society that promotes intellect and rationalization. Because thinking does not happen first, there is no barrier or defense for empaths, they feel everything. This can go to the extreme, where empaths cannot distinguish another person's emotions from their own.

Measuring the Sensitivity of Empaths

Understanding where you fit in the spectrum of empathy is important; because it affects the way you view and interact with the world. There is an exhaustive list of tests that empaths can take to measure their sensitivity. These are intensely interesting to peruse and are quite varied. They vary from questionnaires, reactivity indexes, empathy scales, listening tests, reading emotions tests, and yawning tests—sometimes referred to as the contagious yawning test. The thinking behind the yawning test is that the first person to mimic the yawn is the most empathic of the group.

These tests are usually carried out by trained personnel and can take the form of online, written, observation, and peer assessments. There is also a wide range of self-tests that one can take to get a bit more clarity on which part of the spectrum they fall. Theorists behind these tests date back to 1934 and include the likes of Piaget. Researches look at who is qualified to administer the various tests and how that would affect the outcomes. They need to consider how one can measure empathy and if so, what unit of measurement should be used.

It is interesting to note that there are many tests that are specifically designed for doctors to take to measure their empathy. It is an ability that is needed in order to empathize with ill people. The '*Carkhuff and Truax Empathy Scale*' was designed by Dustin K. MacDonald and is cited below:

"Level 1: Low Level of Empathic Responding

Communicating little or no awareness or understanding of the caller's feelings
Responses are irrelevant or abrasive
Changing the subject, giving advice, etc.

Level 2: Moderately Low Level of Empathic Responding

Responding to the surface message of the caller but omitting feelings or factual aspects of the message.

Inappropriately qualifying feelings (e.g., "somewhat," "a little bit, "kind of")
Inaccurately interpreting feelings (e.g., "angry," "hurt," "tense," or "scared").
Level 2 responses are only partially accurate, but they show an effort to understand.

Level 3: Interchangeable or Reciprocal Level of Empathic Responding

Verbal and nonverbal responses at level 3 show understanding and are essentially interchangeable with the client's obvious expressions, accurately reflecting the client's story and surface feelings or state of being.

Level 4: Moderately High Level of Empathic Responding

Somewhat additive, accurately identifying the client's implicit underlying feelings and/or aspects of the problem.

Volunteer's response illuminates subtle or veiled facets of the client's message, enabling the client to get in touch with somewhat deeper feelings and unexplored meanings and purposes of behavior.

Level 4 responses thus are aimed at enhancing self-awareness.

Level 5: High Level of Empathic Responding

Reflecting each emotional nuance, and using voice and intensity of expressions finely attuned to the client's moment-by-moment experiencing, the volunteer accurately responds to the full range and intensity of both surface and underlying feelings and meanings

A volunteer may connect current feelings and experiencing to previously expressed experiences or feelings, or may accurately identify implicit patterns, themes, or purposes.

Responses may also identify implicit goals embodied in the client's message, which point out a promising direction for personal growth and pave the way for action.

Responding empathically at this high level facilitates the client's exploration of feelings and problems in much greater breadth and depth than responding at a lower level"

Types of Empaths

There are different types of empaths that each portrays a particular strength. The number of types of empaths varies according to the study, article, or doctor. We will look at three of the most common types. While there may be one particular type that you gravitate towards, you can also identify with some aspects of the others. A general understanding of all the types will help you understand how empaths engage and react to the world around them. There are generally three categories which most empaths can fall into. These are the *Physical Empaths*, the *Emotional Empaths*, and the *Intuitive Empaths*.

Physical Empaths

Physical Empaths tend to relate to other people's physical indicators and absorb them

into their bodies. They can either be drained or energized by the other person. These empaths usually become healers of some kind, as they use their ability to sense what is wrong with the other person. Physical empaths need to learn how to control their own energy fields so that they can turn it off when dealing with ailments.

Emotional Empaths

Similarly, Emotional Empaths connect with other people's emotions and absorb them, whether they are joyful or sorrowful. This is one of the most common types of empaths that you will find. For these empaths, it is important to distinguish between one's own emotion and that of others.

Intuitive Empaths

Intuitive Empaths are by far the most interesting. They have amazing super senses like telepathy, intuition, interpreting messages through dreams, synchronicity with nature and one of the increasing popular empaths are the Medium Empaths, who have the ability to connect with the other side. These empaths are finely tuned in with the environment and can read people's energy.

Understanding which type of empath you or your loved one is can help you prevent feeling drained or exhausted and also help you to make the most of your abilities.

How Empaths Interact with Others

Empaths will react to and with the world in different ways, depending on whether they are introverted or extroverted. Introverts are generally considered shy people because they are more involved with their own ideas and emotions rather than with external matters. And similarly, introverted empaths do not have a high threshold for socializing with large groups of people or for the sake of. They prefer the company of people they know and need an exit strategy as they can feel overstimulated after some time. Introverted empaths need to find ways to slow down and re-center.

In contrast, extroverts are socially confident and outgoing people. Extrovert empaths, by nature, are more focused on external matters. They are more vocal and engaging than their introverted counterparts. They enjoy socializing and being around people. These situations do not exhaust or overstimulate them.

Advantages of Being an Empath

Intuition – being intuitive with the flow of energy of people and nature allows one to feel things fully and be totally immersed in experiencing life.

Compassion – empaths are the most considerate and thoughtful people you will find. They are always ready to help others. They dream of the perfect future.

Creative – most empaths are so in tune with themselves that they are able to be creative and see more than others.

Loyalty – empaths make the best friends as they are fiercely loyal and it would take a lot for them to give up on someone.

Nature – empaths are synchronized with nature. Being surrounded by water rejuvenates them. They form special bonds with animals and often rescue them.

Disadvantages of Being an Empath

Overstimulation – empaths feel exhaustion more easily if they do not take time out for themselves. They easily suffer from sensory overload.

Absorbing negativity – empaths relate to the feelings of others so closely that it becomes difficult to differentiate their feelings from those of others. This can cause emotional or physical symptoms to manifest in them.

Compassion – the ability to feel things so closely to those of others can also be a disadvantage. Negative things of this world can be difficult to shake off and can bring them down. They feel the full weight of the pain and suffering of others.

Over stimulation – experiencing sensory overload can take time to get over.

Loneliness –sometimes empaths feel the need to be alone so often that they tend to isolate people from their lives. They may come across as being anti-social when they are trying to look out for themselves.

Exploitation – sometimes people can take advantage of the giving and compassionate nature of empaths.

Sensory overload – coping with loud people, business, noises, and smells can be very daunting for people, whereas some empaths are energized by the full moon, or snowfalls, or thunderstorms.

Expressing needs – needs of intimate relationships can be difficult to articulate. In intimate relationships, not all partners can appreciate an empaths' need for space, or not wanting to share a bed.

Hopefully, this chapter has given you a greater insight into what it means to be an empath.

Chapter Three: How to Have Healthy Relationships

Despite all that we have said thus far about some empaths not being able to be around people for long periods of time, it is possible for empaths to enjoy healthy, positive, and intimate relationships with others. The right balance in a relationship can actually be empowering to empaths. But as always, there are certain things that they need to be aware of to avoid unhealthy dynamics in relationships.

Challenges That Empaths Face in Intimate Relationships

Many empaths will admit to wanting to be a recluse at times. Sometimes they need to be alone like they need to breathe and this can be very hurtful to a partner. As a result, many empaths avoid getting into relationships and remain single for most of their lives. However, being an empath does not mean that one has to relegate themselves to the abyss of loneliness or have a series of short-term relationships. Once you recognize that you are an empath and understand the emotions you feel, as well as why you are feeling them, you can find ways to create the harmony and balance you seek. You will know how to protect yourself from others and not get lost in a relationship or have to endure traumatic relationships. We will deal with ways to protect yourself later in *Chapter Seven*.

Being with someone for long periods of time can be overwhelming to an empath. As much as you may want to experience the joy of being in a relationship, it can get a bit too much. Many empaths run for the hills and leave relationships when this happens. Not recognizing your needs as an empath can make one feel suffocated in relationships and lead to its destruction. Being an empath does not have to mean being alone, it just means that you and your partner will need to adjust to your particular needs. Recognizing the need for an alone time by both partners can lead to a beautiful love experience. This time will refill you and ultimately enhance the relationship and not take away from it. It is important that this time apart is not taken personally, because it is rather paradoxical, you have a need to feel loved and have companionship, but are also afraid of being engulfed and overwhelmed by the relationship. Many empaths unknowingly circumvent getting into relationships because this aspect of absorbing energies and emotions are not understood, and result in solitude. Recognizing the need to take care of yourself in a relationship is very important to the sustainability of any relationship.

Being honest about your 'energy' needs is crucial to the longevity of a relationship. If one is not verbal about these needs, it will eventually become unbearable. The empath will seek a space of little to no stimulation, preferably in nature somewhere, before feeling comfortable within themselves again. Setting boundaries and understanding the energy needs of an empath gives intimate relationships potential. In some cases, traditional models of coupledom may have to change, it all depends on the specific space and time apart—needs that an empath requires. This varies according to personalities, upbringing, culture, and environment.

Empaths are very good at recognizing and expressing their feelings quicker than others. This can be very daunting in a relationship and make them seem like "*know it all's*" and breed resentment. The certainty that an empath has about what he/she feels is unshakeable, and can lead to arguments in relationships and even end them.

Empaths can also come across as being very temperamental because everything they feel is intensified, whether it is joy or anger. Empaths will pick up when a person is lying or not being true to their feelings and will be quite vocal about this not to cause conflict, but because they care. All of these aspects can be difficult to live with when you are in a close relationship.

Why Empaths Make the Best Partners

Embarking on a long-term relationship with an empath can be daunting and filled with challenges from the onset. But let's face it, which relationships are all roses? All relationships require work, effort, and sacrifices for them to progress. However, being in a relationship with an empath can be one of the most rewarding experiences one can have. If scientifically, we know that the empaths' brains are designed to discern the emotions and thoughts of others, then they are the best people to truly and fully understand their partners. Loyalty, compassion, respect, care, love, and understanding will come in leaps and bounds; respecting, understanding, and accepting the needs of an empath can transform a relationship into one full of devotion and mutual love towards each other.

Reasons to Be in a Relationship with an Empath

Empaths are natural healers and caregivers.
They do it for the joy it brings to others and in return feel that joy. Empaths cannot tolerate people experiencing pain; they will do what they can to ease it.

Empaths are fiercely loyal to the people they love and trust.
They will go through leaps and bounds for the other person to make them feel loved and content.

Empaths can spread joy and happiness.
This can infect the people that they are surrounded by. Being in a loving relationship will exponentially increase this sense of joy which in turn will spread to their partners.

Empaths extremely genuine about what they say and do.
Being wired to sense feelings and thoughts make them that way. Because of this, empaths love unconditionally and understand the needs of their partners.

Empathic people have empathy!
Instead of being angry and reacting, they will try to understand, this makes them far more loving and peaceful in nature.

Empaths are natural optimists.
It is a survival strategy against all the negativity of the world. Being with an empath

means you will always get to see the brighter side of things.

Empaths have the innate ability to inspire others and change the world.
They can affect positive change the partners that they are in a relationship with.

Empaths are so in tune with emotions and feelings.
Because of that, they are honest and open about them. This gives an empath's partner security in knowing where they stand. An empath will not play games with someone's emotions and will always be kind and thoughtful.

Empaths are creative because they are so in tune with the world.

This makes them good at solving problems and finding solutions for people and situations.

Empaths are able to connect with others on a much deeper level.
They are so in tune with energies and feelings to the point where they are unable to distinguish it from their own. Being in a relationship with an empath will mean that you will always be understood.

Once an empath falls in love with a person it will be unconditionally.
They will accept all the failings as well as the merits of that person.

For those empaths that still feel that they should shy away from intimate relationships, it must be noted that coupledom is not for everyone. So instead of sabotaging potential relationships, it is better to understand and accept this.

Dealing with Family and Friends

Intimate relationships are not the only kinds of relationships that empaths struggle with. They can struggle with friendships and with family members as well. Personal space needs to be recognized and negotiated depending on the nature of the relationship. In public spaces, not having enough personal space can be suffocating to an empath. Empaths can find creative ways to keep the physical distance from others, like using your trolley in queues so that people don't get too close, or putting your handbag on the seat next to you so that no one sits there. With friends and family, it can be a little trickier.

You have to ensure that you don't offend anyone. To do this, you must be clear that it is not about not loving them and not a personal thing. Being able to articulate these needs will go a long way to creating lasting relationships, rather than you pulling disappearing acts every time you feel emotionally drained. Once you identify the emotional boundary you need, communicating it to others will be much easier. Your relationships with others will flourish and you will not have to feel smothered and avoid them. This negotiation will benefit all parties involved.

Empaths and Narcissists

Firstly, an *empath* is someone who feels an innate need to help and heal others. A *narcissist* is someone who cannot put the needs of others first and are very self-involved. As a result, a narcissist and an empath can often result in toxic relationships. However, narcissists and empaths do have a lot in common. They both recognize the emotional needs and motivations of people. This gives them insight into the insecurities of people. A narcissist will use this information to their own gains whereas an empath will use this information to try and help the other person. So it is easy to see how this will not bode well in a relationship.

The truth is that many narcissists and empaths are drawn to each other because they reflect each other's vices. An empath struggles with feeling dismissed and lost, while a narcissist struggles with obligation and weakness. Empaths, who do not understand themselves fully, will enter these relationships because they believe that love will conquer all. They give off themselves selflessly and to their own detriment. They have no boundaries and become emotionally dependent on the narcissist. Narcissists are often not in touch with their feelings and lack empathy; they would rather see this as a weakness that must be controlled. Narcissists, therefore, seek out empaths as the means through which they can express themselves.

This does not mean that narcissists and empaths should never enter relationships with each other. If the empath recognizes and sets boundaries, there will not be room for a narcissist to manipulate and abuse them. Narcissists need to be forced to deal with and recognize their feelings, and they will start to deal with the root cause of the problem, rather than just project their feelings onto others. The most important thing for narcissists and empaths in a relationship is to be aware of themselves and manage and control their own feelings and behaviors and avoid blaming each other. Being aware of and accepting one's vices will transform into positive aspects, and this awareness can propel narcissists and empaths into productive and progressive relationships. They can then use their high emotional intelligence to realize their potential and live full, happy lives.

Relationship Advice for Empaths

Being in a mutually respectful and loving relationship is important so we have some advice for an empath embarking on this journey.

It is important to express the need for your emotional and personal space early on in the relationship. If the person understands this need, then it bodes well for the relationship. However, if the person puts you down for expressing this need, then the warning bells should go off. The need for space can take different forms, sometimes it can just be a stroll around the block by yourself, other times it could be a weekend getaway—alone.

Some empaths cannot share a bed with a partner. A potential partner needs to understand this need for uninterrupted space and not see it as a rejection of any sort. Energies will mix when sleeping, so to some empaths, this can cause restless sleep. Partners need to understand this and let go of the traditional pattern of coupledom. For some relationships, this could mean sleeping in separate rooms or sleeping apart for a few nights or just separate beds in the same room.

It is crucial for empaths to be honest about their anxieties and what they feel. This will aid in any misunderstandings and can bring couples closer together, as well as allow the partner to play a supportive role. Just as much as an empath needs to be heard, they should also listen to their partners. This way, compromises can be made—if needed—and will create the emotional freedom that healthy relationships need.

Chapter Four: How to Be a Parent as an Empath

It can be particularly challenging for empaths to be parents. Since they absorb everything that their child feels, it can leave them feeling exhausted. Raising empathic children can also be overwhelming. They do not fully understand their sensitivities yet. There are guidelines and techniques to help parents who are raising empaths, to ensure all children are nurtured and developed to their fullest capabilities.

Parenting

If empaths connect so deeply with people's feeling and emotions, can you imagine the extent that this would go to with their own children? Children of empaths would probably have the best childhoods ever. Children of empaths feel loved, taken care of, supported, and heard. Their parents are very much in tune with how they feel and what they need. Parenting as an empath can be a very different experience. Imagine absorbing every emotion of your child? Feeling anxious when they cry, feeling pain when they are rejected, the stress of not wanting them to be hurt in any way, and wanting to protect them from the world. This can lead to significant stress levels.
Being attuned to your offspring puts you on super alert to everything they feel. Sometimes it is worse for you than them.

Emotions can sway from the broodiness of teenagers to the hyper-activeness of toddlers. This rollercoaster is enough to send any parent over the edge—but so much more so for empathic parents. The weight of carrying all those emotions can sit on you for a long time. It seems like there is no escape and that as a parent, all the responsibility lies within you. Empathic parents blame themselves for being too involved and are accused of being too anxious and worrying too much. You either admire or look at other parents in horror by how laid back they may be. Empathic parents are often '*burned out'* and exhausted. The good news is that empathic parents are more likely to raise healthier and happier children and that there are ways to protect yourself from '*burning out'*.

Some characteristics of parents that are empaths are hyper-vigilance and stress. While to some this may seem like an anxiety disorder, it stems from concern for one's child. Being super aware of potential dangers can be exhausting and can also make you seem tense. This long-term stress is not good for the body, mind, and soul. Constantly putting your children's needs before your own can leave you mentally, emotionally, and physically fatigued.

Despite the automatic urge to constantly put your children first, you have to learn how to stop doing that. You have to learn how to take care of yourself first so that you can be your best for them. The basic foundation is to develop emotional resilience.

Research shows that you can do this in three ways:

You have to learn how to be calm.

The minute you trigger stress by worrying about your child, you need to stop and breathe. This activates your parasympathetic nervous system, which counters the sympathetic nervous system—our stress response. When you feel nervous, you start to breathe faster. When you consciously slow your breathing down, your body gets all the signals to calm itself. Inhaling increases your heart rate, exhaling decreases the heart rate. So by lengthening the time between breaths will slow your heart rate, and in turn, calm you down.

Develop self-compassion.

The next step is one of the most underutilized of techniques. Developing self-compassion will improve your physical and psychological well-being. Self-compassion can give you strength. It involves being kind to yourself. Less self-criticism and more kindness are needed. We need to remind ourselves that no one needs to be perfect and that everyone makes mistakes. We can give comfort and encouragement easily to others, but not necessarily ourselves. Basically, we need to use more empathy on ourselves. Being mindful of your thoughts and feelings will help to stand back from it and look at them objectively. This way you don't have to give in to a flood of emotions or deny them.

Give yourself some alone time.

The third step has been touched on earlier in the chapter—alone time. Empaths need this time to rejuvenate themselves. Separation from your children may seem counter-intuitive and even painful, but it is necessary. This can be as simple as taking a relaxing bath, reading a book or taking a walk by yourself.

It is important to practice all these techniques regularly to avoid mental and emotional fatigue. Practice will make regulating intense feelings easier to do. It will also strengthen the emotional resilience you need to flourish as a parent. This, in turn, will filter to your child, making them feel even more secure. The most important thing to remember is to keep the balance between self-care and enjoying the feeling of relating so closely to your offspring.

Nurturing Empathic Children

You do not have to be an empath to give birth to empathic children. And you do not have to be an empath to raise healthy, balanced, empathic children. Just like how adult empaths sense and feel things so intensely, so do empathic children. The difficulty is that children do not know yet how to handle the emotions they feel, so this becomes exponentially more difficult for empathic children. Their nervous systems react more intensely to external stimuli which can lead to sensory overload very quickly. They may respond more intensely to certain smells, bright lights, and noisy spaces. They may prefer certain perfumes, softer fabrics, being in nature etc. Empathic parents can help these children identify triggers and provide solutions to these emotions since they are not able to express or understand the intensity themselves. This will help them deal with it and minimize any discomfort.

As parents of empathic children, you need to know your children well. You need to know what over stimulates them and how to prevent those situations. This will help keep them calm, relaxed, and avoid tantrums. Some common triggers for empathic children are:

- Keeping them busy, filling their days with tasks and activities with no breaks
- Violent programs particularly at night
- Multi-tasking
- No time alone or apart from others

When exposed to the above situations, you may find it harder to get your child to fall asleep. They may need more time to unwind. Parents of empathic children need to remember that their children do not have the same ability to filter out noise, light, and chaos, unlike other children. They may cry or confine themselves to solitude. Certain stimuli can even be painful to them, like cheering and clapping. These sounds will disturb them as opposed to the calming sounds of water and nature.

As much as there are scientific evidence and research, many schools are not equipped to identify or understand empathic children. They are often labeled as anti-social, shy, or fussy. Their quiet, compassionate, and deep nature can give the impression that they are just reserved. In extreme cases, they get diagnosed with a disorder, depression, anxiety, or phobias. It is important for parents to arm themselves with knowledge and solutions in order to help environments like schools make life easier for empathic children. Combatting these misperceptions with tools and awareness will help empathic children and their caregivers cope with the world.

Parents and caregivers should also remember that these children feel and absorb the joy and pain of those around them and can experience emotional discomfort from these situations. Whatever the adult feels, it will be intensified for the child.

There are many people who do not understand what empaths are, let alone how to respond to them. When empathic children are dismissed as being 'overly sensitive' and told to 'grow thicker skin' they are made to feel like there is something wrong with them.

They will feel misunderstood and start to withdraw from people. It is important for us to increase the awareness and support of empathic children in understanding their unique qualities.

How to Know If Your Child Is an Empath?

Recognizing whether or not your child is an empath is the first step to helping your child live the best that they can be. Once this is established, a parent can support them in the way that is required. Below are some traits of empathic children:

- They have intense emotions.
- They get quickly over-stimulated when they are around crowds and noise.
- They have strong reactions to sad books or scary movies.

- They often want to leave family gatherings early or just be by themselves.
- They think they are different from other children.
- They are very good at listening to people.
- They amaze you with intuitive or insightful comments that you would not expect from a child.
- They have a particular affinity for nature and animals.
- They get upset when other children have been mistreated or victimized.
- They have a few good friends, rather than a large circle of friends.

The more your child can relate, the stronger their empathic inclinations are. It is important to nurture these children as they have the abilities needed to solve the cruel world we live in. they need to learn to appreciate their sensitivities and nor resent them.

Chapter Five: How to Thrive in the World of Work as an Empath

One of the things we spent a huge amount of time doing is our jobs or occupations. Finding the right job for an empath is like the difference between a happy fulfilled life and a frustrated one. Privacy is difficult to get in many work environments with many open-plan office spaces. Being constantly surrounded by people can leave an empath feeling very overwhelmed. It is important, especially for empaths, to find environments that suit their temperament or learn how to set boundaries and learn how to center themselves at work.

Empaths are naturally driven to make the world a better place. They share a strong desire to help people and often sacrifice themselves in the process. It is, therefore, important for empaths to find work that is meaningful to them, that will make a positive impact on the lives of others. They tend to stay away from competitive careers and those driven by money. Careers in the healing field like teaching and counseling appeal more to empaths.

A Changing Work Environment

It is becoming an increasing ten in the workplace for empaths to be placed on emotional quotient, rather than intelligence quotient. Humanity or empathy is becoming more of a priority, as well as a social responsibility. It seems that empaths are starting to make their mark on the world after all.

Companies that can develop an empathic culture are the ones that thrive. When you can step into someone else's shoes and relate to them genuinely, they feel appreciated and give so much more and are much more loyal. Empaths can offer much to the work environment because they genuinely care; however, if they do not protect themselves, they can succumb to exhaustion and feeling overwhelmed. More empaths are needed in the workplace. Research shows that productivity is on the decline when employees feel that their managers do not care about them and the work that they do. Workers feel that their employers are out of touch with what happens on the ground and remain aloof in the confinement of boardrooms and presentations.

Emotional contagion was discussed earlier in the book. One can see how dangerous this could be to a work environment. It can affect the morale of the staff if it is negative. However, the opposite can be said if it is a positive, happy, and productive work environment.

In today's work environments, there is not much space between co-workers, so it makes it difficult for an empath to avoid the stimulation from others. An empath can hear others around them gossiping, complaining, coughing, and laughing. They can smell the odors of the people around them. This sensory overload can be hugely stressful to empaths.

Some progressive companies have recognized the need of their employees, and provide creative and alternative spaces for their employees to perform at their best. You now find couches in some workplaces, designated quiet spaces for those that need it.

It is not always possible to control the environment you find yourself in, but you can learn some techniques to help you cope. There are ways to minimize emotional contagion and to create a safe, pleasant workspace for yourself. The first thing you need to do is understand energy.

There are colleagues who will energize empaths, and there are colleagues who will make empaths feel like they suck the life out of them. The relationship you have with these people will ultimately affect your physical well-being. It is important to thrive in a working environment where you can recognize these different types of people, and learn how to navigate your way around them to prevent fatigue and resentment. It is important to create an environment where you can feel safe and happy.

Empaths need to limit the time they set aside to listen to other people, especially if these are mainly complaints. It helps to have exit lines ready to use like "*I'm sorry, I have many deadlines to meet today, I only have a few minutes to spare*" or politely change the topic. Some co-workers do not respond to verbal or nonverbal cues, and you have to approach the problem more directly. It is important to recognize any triggers and respond calmly and rationally. If these do not work, you can try visualization—putting yourself in a happier more serene space where the negativity the co-worker brings does not affect you. By looking at the people you need to be in contact with and the ways that they affect you, you can find strategies to help you deal with them. Setting limits and implementing them is the key when it comes to people who will upset your emotional well-being.

A workplace can either drain all your energy and motivation away or energize and nourish you. Obviously, it is the latter we all aspire to, as it will create an environment that fosters creativity and passion. The former will probably find an empath staying away from work, feeling sick often, and constantly feel emotional stress.

Since work and careers play such a momentous part of our lives, it is important to create the right environment. Achieving this is twofold, you have to find meaning and purpose in your job, and you have to understand and manage the energy of the space and people around you.

Understanding Energy

Everything on earth has its own vibration and therefore its own energy. For empaths, energy becomes a primary means of communication. Plants, animals, people, and even water have a vibration or frequency that is unique to it. This is what defines their existence in the universe. This knowledge is based on scientific evidence that is documented. You can actually see these vibrations and frequencies in brain scans and other energy graphs.

Negative energy attracts more negative energy and positive attracts positive energy. Energy can also repel each other. Empaths and non-empaths can consciously use this energy if they are aware of it. Some people send out positive energy and you feel refreshed around them. Other people absorb positive energy and leave people around them feeling drained. The minute one starts to pay attention to this aspect, you will notice it more and more. There are some people that are just more charismatic and attract you to them. Think about dynamic leaders and how you feel after being in their presence.

An empath is affected by the energy that is emitted from others. People may not be aware of the emotional frequencies that they send out. When an empath picks up on this, they will have an emotional or physical response to it. The more enlightened you are as an empath, the quicker and easier it is to do this. An untrained empath is vulnerable to these and will be affected more intensely. Walking into a boardroom or networking session can easily turn into a nightmare for empaths. They may feel overwhelmed and struggle to concentrate and focus. Empaths need to become aware of the people that feed off their energy, this can happen in the first moments of coming into contact with that person. This difference in energy needs can lead to stress and a breakdown in the relationship. Highly stressful situations at work can be avoided if empaths learn how to block the emotions or energies that they are feeling. Most of the time, people are unaware of their energy frequencies and do not realize the effect it has on others. It is important for empaths to train themselves on how to cope with various situations and predicaments, and thereby, shield themselves from unnecessary and debilitating stress.

Creating Boundaries

It is important to create physical and emotional boundaries around yourself at work. Not all of us have the mental fortitude of gurus and monks, so the good news is that empaths can also use some physical objects in their environment to help them in this regard. These may serve more as a psychological barrier but it will help with your state of mind.

If you find yourself in a modern day open plan office space, where you do not enjoy the space that your desk provides, you can create a type of barrier around you.
By this, I mean a physical barrier with small plants, photos or precious stones.
Create emotional distance from people by using earphones that cut off sound and noise.

You can take breaks or a walk to get fresh air.

You can also purify a place by burning scented candles or incense. However, you have to be aware that some co-workers may be uncomfortable with this.

You could do a silent meditation that is not invasive to anyone.

And finally, you can use objects like plants and mirrors to change the energy of the space.

Visualization helps some people. You visualize that your entire workspace is surrounded by light that resists anything negative and only attracts that which is positive. It is a strategy to help you feel protected, and thereby, empower you.

Empaths need to learn how to cope with negative people in the workplace and use whatever means are at their disposal to aid them. How you cope with this at work can affect your comfort levels at work. One has to learn and practice strategies to create the physical, emotional and psychological barriers that are required to create a pleasant work environment. You may not be able to control who you work with, or even the setting you work in, but you can make an effort at shifting the energy you find yourself in. you can use the above strategies to minimize the emotional contagion found in workspaces.

Choosing Careers

When an empath finds the right career for them, they can be invaluable in that field. An empath needs to recognize that their contributions may not be valued in certain fields like the military or corporations, but highly sought after in fields of healthcare, education, and the arts. When choosing a career, an empath needs to consider not just the requirements and skills of a job but also the energy of the environment, and the vision and mission of the company. An empath will need to trust their intuition and instinct when it comes to making a decision, as this requires actively being aware of the energy they sense.

The key factor when choosing a career path is to truly understand and know your capabilities. Compassionate professions can be an excellent career choice initially, but the weight of carrying the pain and the suffering of others can be too much to bear. Trained empaths who can set boundaries, coping techniques, and limits can strive in these fields. Knowing who you are and your limits will help you make the best career choice for you.

The Best Jobs for Empaths

There are certain fields that are naturally inclined towards the best traits of an empath and will provide them with fulfillment and satisfaction.

Many empaths are natural artists. An artist's job is to reflect the world they find themselves in, or comment on it and make others contemplate these ideas, and because empaths are more perceptive and in tune with their environment, they are naturally inclined towards being an artist. The intensity with which they feel and sense the world helps them in creating meaningful art in all forms. Empaths, who choose a field of art, find a way to channel whatever they feel into their art. In return, the world is beautified by these wonderful expressions that move us and inspire us. There are very few artists in the world that get rich by creating their art, so the motivation behind this is more to make an impact on the world and change lives for the better.

Healthcare

The compassionate and caring nature of an empath makes them ideal for an occupation in healthcare. Many empaths become doctors, nurses, and psychologists to fill their need to help others. The most important thing for empaths, as healthcare professionals, is to have techniques and strategies to shield them from taking on too much from their patients.

Social workers deal directly with vulnerable people and children—empaths would naturally gravitate towards this career. They give their time and effort and often work long hours. Their goal is to improve and protect the lives of the people they come into contact with. This career, however, can expose an empath to the harsh and cruel realities of the world; it is imperative that they have strong coping strategies to deal with the pain and suffering that they come across. Not having these strategies in place have caused many social workers to leave their jobs after a few years due to emotional and mental exhaustion.

Many empaths find themselves in hospice work where they provide care and support to families of patients with illnesses. They also provide extra care and support to the patient as the families' may not necessarily be able to cope. Some empaths do this type of work as volunteers, as their day jobs may not fill their need to help others.

At first, one may think to be a lawyer is at odds with who an empath is, but it can be a perfect fit for those who need to champion causes. It is a job where you can serve and help people and make a difference in the world. We generally associate lawyers with expensive fees and being ruthless, but this is a generalization and stereotype. Empaths as lawyers can identify with what their clients feel, and what they are going through, this makes them the best people to represent others, especially those that are abused. There are times that the sensitivities of an empath will fair against them in situations when there are huge conflict and great stress.

Self-employment becomes a choice for many empaths as they can have the flexibility and freedom to choose their work environments. They get to choose their colleagues and clients and can work on their own if they feel the need to. Self-employment also means fewer meetings with groups of people, and that is a huge positive for empaths.

Many businesses have opted for flexi-time and allow employees to work from home and communicate via apps and online platforms. This environment is also suitable to empaths. The disadvantage is that one often ends up working far more than they would at an office. So once again, it becomes important to implement boundaries.

The Worst Jobs for Empaths

Sales jobs are probably one of the worst jobs that an empath can try. This job requires one to deal with all kinds of people and manipulate them into purchasing something that you know deep down they do not really need. This is at complete odds for an empath who seeks to help and enhance the lives of others. A sales job can be emotionally draining for an empath. Being a salesperson in a shop or supermarket can mean that an empath is bombarded by people, noises, loudspeakers, and bright lights all the time. This is the exact opposite description of the ideal environment for an empath.

Customer care and public relations may also be very stressful choices for an empath, as they are careers that involve small talk, being aggressive and agreeable. The corporate world presents problems for an empath as well. There is usually rules and protocols to follow that are non-negotiable and do not value the individual. Empaths are deep thinkers and enjoy thinking out of the box to find solutions. They will speak up if they feel strongly about an issue and won't be swayed easily. This ability may not go down well in all corporate environments, and they can be seen as being difficult. They don't do well with competitive co-workers and can find them draining.

If you do find yourself in one of these careers and no way out, you can find ways to improve your situation. Empaths who are happy at work can be valuable employees.

Chapter Six: Why Some Empaths Turn to Addiction

Many people, even those that are mindful of empaths and non-empaths, are unaware that empaths do not have the tools to cope with what the world throws at them. They do not know how to cope with the feeling of being overwhelmed and turn to negative means of coping with these feelings. Empaths will try to solve or numb what they are feeling by turning to addictions. These can take the form of alcohol, medication, sex, gambling, food etc.

Medication is sometimes the easy go-to when empaths feel the sensory overload, which can lead to anxiety and depression.

This solution deals with the symptoms and not the cause. Empaths need to learn how to shield themselves from the intensity of their emotions, rather than turning to quick-fix solutions.

Empaths also need to learn to accept themselves and realize that they are different from other people and will not cope in the same ways as other people. These can sometimes refer to things that other people take completely for granted. Going to the supermarket at the end of the month or navigating freeways during peak traffic times, can affect empaths intensely. They can feel extreme anxiety by doing these simple day to day activities. Non-empaths will not understand how these events can cause sensory overload and hyper-stimulation for empaths. Breathing exercises do not always help in these situations, and the lack of empathy and understanding from others and themselves can make empaths turn to alternative means, or ways of dealing with what they feel.

Addiction becomes distractions from having to deal with the sensory overload. It takes your attention away from having to deal with the world. Certain addictive substances like medication and alcohol can change the energy or vibration of an empath, either making it higher or lower, putting them in a state where they are not as aware of the sensory input around them. Addictions to running, exercise, or yoga will release endorphins which counter any pain felt because endorphins are associated with feel-good hormones.

Food becomes another way that empaths numb themselves. Foods high in carbohydrates or sugars raise insulin. It is believed that we crave these foods because they raise our dopamine levels. So empaths turn to these foods as a way to counter the depression or sensory overload that they feel.

Many addicts come from homes that are supportive and wealthy—which leave people thinking and pondering about why they became addicts. If what the empaths feel is amplified, then those people are carrying loads of emotional pain, anxiety, loss, and hurt of many. This can be debilitating and it can be difficult to feel upbeat or normal. For the most part, empaths try to keep an emotional balance through alcohol, smoking, and eating addictions, but for others, it is much harder to keep the addiction under control.

For the most part, the addiction is a way to disconnect and to retreat. But no matter how much empaths try to distance themselves from feeling through substances, it does not solve the problem. If anything, it creates more conflicts in our relationships and can cause further frustration, loneliness, and depression. The distance empaths can create can take the following forms:

- Preferring isolation
- Decreased sex drive
- Being emotionally shut off
- Ending relationships

More and more research is beginning to show that the answer to addiction is a connection. By this, I mean that instead of empaths trying to avoid the feelings, they should embrace them fully as a means to release them. One way to do this is by talking about these feelings to someone they trust and that will support. This is the connection!

Medication and Empaths

There are times when trying to deal with the sensory overload can be too overwhelming and medication is needed to combat depression and anxiety. The good news is that since empaths are so sensitive to everything, they are also sensitive to medication, and therefore, require less for it to start showing positive results. Many empaths usually find that traditional doses of medication are difficult for them to tolerate. Many pain medications inhibit empathy and become a go-to drug for empaths who are trying to cope with a barrage of emotions.

Empaths, who need medication, need to find medical practitioners who are sensitive to the sensitivity of empaths and can adjust the dosage accordingly.

Chapter Seven: How to Protect Yourself as an Empath

Empaths need to learn ways and means to protect themselves from toxic people, or when they are around noise, business, and chaos to avoid feeling overwhelmed and exhausted. One of the many abilities of empaths is honing in subtle non-verbal cues, thereby opening themselves up to the feelings and energy of others that are not consciously displayed. This makes empaths good at reading people and situations and knowing when people are being dishonest or not authentic. However, the negative side to these abilities is that it presents the empaths with a host of problems. They can be overwhelmed by energy overload, by absorbing other people's energy. Negative energy can leave an empath feeling disconnected and heavy.

We have spoken in previous chapters about boundaries and setting limits and being assertive. In Chapter Five, we covered aspects of psychological, emotional, and physical barriers that empaths can use to protect themselves. This chapter sums up all the things an empath can do proactively to reduce this sensory onslaught and techniques to get rid of it.

Energy Fields

Every person has invisible sheets of electromagnetic waves that surround them, some people refer to this as their aura, but a more scientific term is '*biofield*'. For non-empaths, this field is well defined and unified. For empaths, it is permeable and fluid. This makes it vulnerable to the penetration of foreign energy. Trained empaths can use this sensitivity to read spaces and people. They can sense when they walk into a room or space and immediately feel if it is tense or welcoming. Places where there is a lot of energy condensed together like shopping malls, schools, and hospitals offer energy overload to empaths and they try to avoid them. As an empath, one has to learn about how energy works, as well as your own personal sensitivities and the type of empath you are. This information will help guide you to the techniques and tools you will need.

Taking Care of Yourself

There are certain rituals that an empath needs to follow to avoid all the negative stuff they are prone to. The first is the little things that they need to do to take care of themselves. Empaths need to be in tune with their vibrations, as it creates the foundation from which they interact with the world. Non-empaths are attracted to the high vibrations of empaths and see them as role models. In this way, empaths can teach others how to be in this world and eliminate many cruelties. When empaths take care of and look after themselves, they will teach others, by example, to do the same. By taking care of themselves first, empaths will be able to blossom and fulfill their purpose in this life, and thereby, make an impact on the world.

Healthy Living

The first step in this process is to look at what we put into our bodies, on our bodies, and what we surround our bodies with.

Things we put into our bodies include *food, medication, and drinks*.

Things we put on our bodies include *clothing, jewelry, etc*.

Things we surround ourselves with include *furniture, household items, even cleaning products*.

All of these things will have an effect on our bodies, and empaths will be more susceptible to its influence. Being aware of the choices an empath makes when purchasing all of these various items must be careful and deliberate. Generally, these items should be organic. Non-organic items have a lower vibration and can negatively affect empaths. Being extremely sensitive means, that empaths must make conscious choices.

Exercise

We release toxins from our bodies through salt. So when empaths cry or sweat, it is actually very good for them. Toxins and negative energy will build up in the body over time, so it is important to release these on a regular basis. If you do not like exercising, you can find creative ways to sweat. Many gyms now offer heated studios for yoga and Pilates. Yoga is designed to release negative energy through meditation, so the combination with sweating makes it an excellent choice. Biking, walking, or running in nature is also very good. Nature has a vibration and can heal you.

Meditation

A great way to clear your mind, discharging negative energy, and reconnecting with yourself is through meditation. Meditation is crucial for empaths, so we have dedicated the entire next chapter to meditation. Meditation does not have to be long and onerous; it can be adapted to the needs and situation. Some empaths prefer to meditate in yoga or outdoors in nature, some prefer guided meditation, and some just prefer to focus on their breathing; for some, it is just some alone time, a place where they can be still. Whichever form appeals to you is the one you should go for. The most important thing is to do it on a regular basis. Quick meditations throughout the day can help an empath stay centered. If an empath feels that their heartbeat is increasing, or a sense of fear and being overwhelmed, they should stop and do a quick meditation to bring them back in charge of their emotional state. These short meditations should not be underestimated, they can be phenomenal.

Good Judgment

Empaths must learn to make good choices. They need to make conscious choices about who they spend their time with, how they spend their time, and where they spend their time. If these choices do not support their purpose in life or higher good, they will not be beneficial to anyone else. An empath can use their gut feelings or intuition to guide them in this regard. When authentic choices are made, toxicity and overload can be eliminated.

Listening to Your Instincts

As has been stated throughout this book, empaths are extremely sensitive. This means being in tune with their senses can make them intuitive. Empaths need to learn how to listen, understand and interpret what their instincts, feelings, and senses are telling them. To do this, empaths need to be very aware of how their bodies respond in different situations. Their intuition will tell them if their energy has increased or decreased when in certain situations or around certain people. With practice, this becomes easier and quicker. To begin with, an empath will have to make a conscious effort to be aware of this intuition or feeling. Then it is important to follow this instinct and stick to people who increase your energy and limit the time you spend with people who decrease your energy. Sometimes intuition can come in the form of dreams, ideas, and thoughts. Intuition will provide signs and guidance but no an explanation. Expressing gratitude also helps an empath to keep at the moment. Expressing gratitude on a regular basis will also increase the positive energy around you.

Spiritual Guidance

Having a spiritual connection provides an opportunity for empaths to experience support, understanding, and unconditional love. This spiritual connection can take any form that is suitable and comfortable for the empath. For some its guardian angels, for some it's prayer. Developing this connection will provide healing and clarity. This connection can even take place during meditations.

Breathing

Mindful breathing is very closely related to meditation. It is basically becoming aware of your breath. You can use this to breathe in positive energy and breathe out negative energy. You will feel the difference in your heart rate and feel calmer. This can be practiced throughout the day and whenever you feel you are in a stressful situation.

A Time Out

This aspect has been covered previously in the book. It is essential to empaths and a deliberate effort to taking time out has to be made. These little breaks of alone time will help to emotionally unwind. A timeout can be as long as you want. It can be an entire weekend away or just a quick walk by oneself.

Some Tips on How to Keep Centered

Empaths are more affected by negative influences than non-empaths. Setting boundaries and sticking to them is vital to your emotional health. It is okay to say "No" to someone if you feel they are asking too much of you. It is okay to put distance between yourself and anything that brings your energy down. Empaths need to do whatever it requires to keep their peace of mind. This may mean limiting one's contact with anything negative—even watching the news or watching horrific and violent programs.

If you know you will be exposed to large groups of people or crowds and you cannot avoid them, plan exit strategies like going to your car or having another means of transportation. Set a limit to the time you will spend there. This should be based on your comfort levels. It helps to eat a high protein meal before the time. This will ground you. You can also stay closer to the perimeter or quieter areas and avoid being in the dead center of a space.

Try not to eat to numb what you are feeling. When feeling

tempted, practice a quick meditation and exercise caution. It also helps to have something near the refrigerator to help remind you in case you unwittingly find yourself at your refrigerator ready to indulge.

You can't always shake off and avoid emotions. Sometimes they need to be addressed. Empaths can learn to manage their emotions by recognizing them and delving into the causes and associations with them. Have honest, realistic conversations with yourself to put these thoughts and feelings into perspective. Realizing where they come from can allow you to recognize them as true feelings, or perhaps there is another way to look at it and minimize your stress.

Develop a routine of cleaning and clearing your spaces. Pay particular attention to your spaces at home and at work, where you would spend most of your time. People turn towards sprays, oils, incense, sage, and feng shui to clear the energy fields around them. This routine should include yoga and other forms of exercise as well.

It is important to learn how to recognize what your needs are. Empaths are generally very sensitive so they need to be aware of the environments that they may find exhausting. They need to be aware of environments where they feel refreshed and rejuvenated. Mastering the balance of the two will enable an empath to function at their best. Empaths need to honor what they need, be it time for contemplation or healing.

It helps to associate with people that are aware and sensitive to the needs of an empath. They can be a support system and help to implement and remind you of the techniques or means you have at your disposal when required.

Taking care of yourself in this way will help you to be better for your friends and family and be a source of joy, comfort, and healing to them.

Tips to Renounce Toxic Energy

Being an empath can be difficult at first. Even if we do practice pro-active regimes to avoid taking on toxic energy, it can still happen. There are things that an empath can do if this does happen.

Here are some tips:

> The first thing to do is to evaluate whether what you are feeling actually does belong to you, or if you have just absorbed someone else's emotions. You need to ask yourself if the anxiety or distress is your own or someone else's. Listening to your intuition is the key to determining this. If these emotions do belong to you, you

need to investigate them further. Try to figure out the cause, speak to a trusted friend or seek counseling if necessary. If these emotions do not belong to you, you need to figure out who they are coming from. Again, you need to hone in and listen to your intuition.

Once you have been able to do this, you need to find a way to politely remove yourself from the source. Once you are able to get about twenty feet away, take note to see if you start to feel any different. In times like these, we want to be polite and not offend people. It is important to put yourself first. Do not hesitate if you need to change seats. With time, you will develop ways to do this easily.

In order to become aware of what our bodies are telling us, we need to take note in these situations where we feel the discomfort. For most empaths, it is usually their stomachs or gut. For others, it may come in the form of headaches, sore throats, and infections. Empaths need to scan their bodies to see which of their body is their vulnerable point or points. When you notice this symptom, the immediate thing you can do is place our hand on the inflicted area and envision ease and comfort to the area. This technique, when practiced daily, can strengthen the area. This technique will provide ease and relaxation.

The next thing an empath can do to remove toxic energy is to remember to use their breather. Focus and concentrate on your breath for a few minutes. This will help to center and ground you and reconnect you to your sense of peace.

Quick and fast meditations—which are sometimes referred to as guerilla mediations—can be executed next. This combats negative emotional and physical symptoms very quickly, in fact, in a matter of minutes, a sense of relief can be achieved. These meditations can be done anywhere. These can be done at parties, conferences, work, or even at home. You just need to find a quiet space like a bathroom and meditate there. The first step is to mindfully calm yourself and then focus on love and positivity.

Visualization often helps empaths. The security that comes from it might only be psychological, but it empowers and gives strength to empaths. Your thoughts will actualize. You can envision yourself surrounded by white protective light or a powerful jaguar keeping guard on you. In moments of vulnerability, empaths must use whatever means possible to protect themselves. The spaces between one's vertebrae contribute to reducing pain in one's body. Visualizing pain out of these areas can provide relief. This is done with conscious thought directed to these areas.

Water is a natural cleanser. Taking a bath or shower is very refreshing and soothing. It is a quick and instant way to dissolve stress, anxiety, and accumulated toxins. Take note of how you feel straight after having taken a bath or shower. Not only do they wash away physical dirt and grime but emotional and psychological ones as well.

It is important for an empath to continue to practices the strategies above regularly. This will help you to create a space where you can be nurtured and restored, as well as respond quicker when you are in a negative space. Empaths do not have to take on the world's burdens; they are meant to thrive, flourish, and spread joy and hope in the world. In order to do this, you must take care of and protect yourself first.

Chapter Eight: The Benefits of Meditation

There may not always be ways and means to block or shut out negative energies or emotions, so it helps to arm oneself with some techniques to protect your own energy field. This will help you to be in control of what affects you. The best and most effective way to do this is through meditation.

Finding inner peace and happiness, less anxiety, more positivity, and joy can be found through the ability to control your mind and thoughts. Learning to control the mind is a prerequisite for empaths to have a happy life. The way you feel about something starts with the thoughts you have. To feel happy and connected you need to start with those thoughts. Therefore, thoughts prompt either positive or negative thoughts. Thoughts can keep you from having a good sleep; they take over when you do something menial like driving and can distract you from living fully in the moment. Being able to still the mind is the most empowering thing for an empath. Learning to gain control over your thoughts will take time, but it is well worth the effort. You can do this through meditation.

Meditation means that empaths can have better control over thoughts that activate negative emotions. Meditation puts you at a place of equilibrium. When you are able to let go of resistance and anxiety, you make way for inner peace and clarity to enter.

Meditations allow you to create the most beneficial starting point for you each day.

Medical Benefits

There are many benefits, besides those specific to empaths that will benefit someone that meditates. Meditation will also improve your immune function and enhance your physical health. Meditation lowers stress levels, anxiety and improves the quality of your breathing. When we learn the benefits of meditation, we will see that it becomes a means to cope with a range of physical disorders and cognitive challenges without the need to take medication. The emotional and health-boosting benefits are based on scientific evidence that can be found everywhere if one bothers to look.

Meditation, when done in the dark, is more beneficial. The darkness helps to keep the pineal gland in good shape, which then positively affects the production of melatonin. Melatonin is produced by the pineal gland when in darkness, is considered the anti-aging hormone that the body produces naturally. So yes, meditation will help in anti-aging, de-stressing, and help you to sleep better. Those who suffer from insomnia or have mild sleeping difficulties are believed to have a melatonin deficiency. Melatonin does not just help to regulate sleep, it is an antioxidant, anti-inflammatory, and prevents and treats many illnesses including cancer. It is well known that the immune system does most of its work at night and that it is believed to be linked to the production of melatonin. We need to spend more time in darkness to produce melatonin. However, modern-day living does not always allow for this. We have street lights and sheer curtains so our bedrooms are letting light in. this reduces the production of melatonin and affects a person's sleep. Meditating before you sleep in complete darkness will aid the production of melatonin. This, together with the ability of meditation to stimulate the pineal gland is proof of the numerous benefits of meditating.

The Basics

Peace of mind and controlling one's thoughts are not just the only benefits to mediation. One has to set time aside every day to practice meditation. It does require commitment and dedication. One should start with a few minutes each day and increase it gradually. People do not have to meditate for hours to reap the benefits. It is important to choose a space where there will be no disturbance. This is trickier to achieve in a household with small children, but with a little negotiation, it can be achieved. To tune out external noise, one can play some gentle, soothing music to meditate to. There is also a myriad of guided meditations that one can purchase and listen to. It is important to have a regular routine before the rewards can be reaped.

Effective Release

Meditation is an exceptionally valuable practice to use to overturn negative thinking that leads to a buildup of stress and anxiety. A quick Google search will lead you to a myriad of studies that show the beneficial effects of meditation. In a 2009 meditation study, researchers at UCLA found that parts of the brain that regulate emotion were considerably larger in long-term practitioners of meditation than those who do not practice meditation. High-resolution magnetic resonance imaging (MRI) was documented that measured the size of areas in the brain such as the hippocampus, the thalamus, and lower temporal gyrus. Researchers noted that people who consistently meditate are able to develop positive emotions, maintain emotional constancy and engage in mindful activities. The participants of this study meditated on average between ten and one and a half hours each day.

Types of Meditation

There are many types of meditation to suit each type of empath. These range from visualization, chanting, breath-work, and trance. Meditation does not have to be indoors. You can meditate while walking by focusing your awareness on the things around you. This could be like the way your feet feel on grass, or how the sunlight feels on your skin. Some of the most common types are outlined below:

Metta Meditation

The goal of this type is to develop an outlook of love and kindness even towards negativity and stress-generating triggers. It is a very useful meditation for empaths who come across energy zappers at work or at family gatherings. During meditation, practitioners send out *loving kindness* to specific people, their families, and friends and to the world in general. With continued regular practice, it will become easier for an empath to incorporate the perspective of *loving kindness* into a habit. An outlook of *loving-kindness* promotes compassion towards oneself and towards others and is especially helpful to remove feelings of anger, frustration, and resentment, while at the same time promoting positive emotions.

Body Scan or Progressive Relaxation

This is a good meditation for empaths trying to learn what their bodies are telling them. It helps empaths to find out where their vulnerable points are, and will help to reduce the effects of negativity and overload in the long term. During this type of meditation, practitioners are required to scan their bodies to identify areas of tension. Once tension is identified, through focus and intention, the tension is released first from one area and then the next. One can start the scan from the feet upwards or from the head down. It is important to give attention to every part of the body. The effects of progressive relaxation encourage relaxation and feelings of peace. It helps empaths to get to a place of equilibrium. It can also be useful to help those who suffer from chronic pain to cope more effectively and to sleep better.

Mindfulness Meditation

One of the most common *mindfulness meditation* prompts meditators to remain present, aware, and in the moment. One has to avoid thinking of the past or future. This is difficult to achieve, but with perseverance comes success. One has to take note of his/her surroundings. This includes noting sights, sounds and smells without attaching any judgment. One of the reasons why mindfulness is so popular is that it can be practiced anywhere and at any time: in the queue at the bank, in the garden, on a walk, and while waiting for the kettle to boil. This type of meditation is useful to empaths because it is so versatile. More scientific research has been invested in the benefits of *mindfulness meditation* because it is so widely practiced. The benefits include reducing the impact of negative thoughts, improving focus and concentration, and reducing emotional reactions to people and situations. All the things an empath needs to conquer.

Breath Awareness Meditation

This is a subcategory of the mindfulness meditation practice that focuses on conscious breathing. Meditators can either count deep and slow breaths, or they just pay attention to the inhale and exhale of each breath. All other thoughts are quieted by ignoring it or telling the brain to refocus. This type of meditation is particularly useful for reducing anxiety and is therefore beneficial to empaths. It is also a meditation that can be practiced anywhere making it useful when one notices a trigger is activated.

Kundalini Yoga

Kundalini yoga is a form of meditation that harmoniously combines movement with incantations and deep breathing. Practitioners usually attend a class led by a teacher. The other popular option is to follow a video or DVD. The benefits include enhanced physical strength and improved positive mental health. These are aspects that empaths need to strengthen and add to their arsenal of protection.

Zen Meditation

A Zen meditation, or Zazen as it is also referred to, is a type of meditation that belongs to the Buddhist practice. Like Kundalini yoga, this practice is composed of specific steps and dedicated postures. Once in a comfortable position, the practitioner pays attention to the breath and observes thought without judging the thinking pattern. If one is struggling with eliminating thoughts, this may be a good meditation to start with. For those empaths that are more physical and need to move, this will also help make the meditation more relaxing.

Transcendental Meditation

For empaths looking for a more devoted spiritual form of meditation, transcendental meditation is a popular option. Meditators are seated comfortably and breathe in and out slowly. Meditators can either concentrate on a mantra that is already determined by a teacher, or of their own choosing such as a positive affirmation. This is a powerful meditation not just to get off toxic and negative energy, but also to strengthen one's empathic abilities.

It is important to find what works for you. It is imperative to be kind, patient, and loving towards yourself rather than criticizing yourself for not doing it right. Self-care and self-love are vital for empaths to thrive. You will know you're on the right track when you begin to feel the amazing benefits that a calm and relaxed mind will bring into your life, and when you can start using your skills to benefit the lives around you.

If meditation is a completely unfamiliar practice to you then here are a few tips to becoming a pro at it.

Tips for Successful Meditation:

Choose a comfortable quiet spot to sit or lie down. There must be nothing that will distract you from your meditated state. All hones should be switched off. The family needs to be told that this is your time and that they cannot disturb you. Using headphones will help to shut out the background noise.

Meditating is better with your eyes closed. If you can't manage this, switch off the lights, or if you're meditating during the day, use eye masks. Start off slow and easy with just a few minutes and slowly increase the duration as you become proficient at meditation.

Start by counting down from 10 and repeat this until you feel relaxed.

Do not judge yourself or get annoyed if thoughts start to enter your mind. Gently dismiss them and refocus. This may happen many times over so be prepared for that. It is completely natural in the beginning. Everyone experiences this; it will get better with time and practice. Listening to gentle, soothing music during a meditation helps with focus. One has to pay close attention to the notes of the music. Thoughts will filter in, they are persistent. Without criticism, gently push them aside and remind yourself to refocus.

Another very useful tip often used in meditations is to deliberately place awareness on each part of the body. See and feel light entering the brain and moving down from the head to the face, to the neck and shoulders, and slowly progressing through the body until it reaches the toes. This may not be a timed technique, but it is much easier to focus on and less of a chance of intruding thoughts entering your mind.

If meditation does not quite resonate with you, you can try mindfulness practices that suit your personality and lifestyle:

Mindfulness

This is a practice where you try to remain in the moment and aware of where you are and your experience. One needs an object to anchor their experience. The most common choice is breath, but it could be a sound, a visual or a physical object that helps to encourage mental strength.

Yoga

For those who struggle to sit still and focus, yoga may be the answer. Yoga is the combination of movement with awareness; it reconnects the body, mind, and spirit.

Breathing from the Abdomen

Breathing grounds you and helps to relieve symptoms of stress and anxiety. People mostly take shallow breaths and breathe quite rapidly. One has to learn to slow this process down and breathing from your lungs instead of your chest. As you do this, you will notice that your stomach inflates as you inhale and deflates as you exhale. Initially, one might experience being light-headed, if this happens, stop until you feel normal again before continuing. This type of breathing should be done for a few minutes each to release feelings of tension, stress, and anxiousness.

Breathing from the Nostrils

Another good technique is to breathe from alternate nostrils. It is important to be in a comfortable position, sitting upright, and keeping your eyes closed. The right thumb is positioned on the right nostril, and the right ring finger will linger over the left nostril. When the right nostril is closed, one needs to inhale through the left for three seconds. Thereafter, close the left nostril and breathe through the right nostril for three seconds. This process needs to be repeated for about twenty times. Do not be alarmed if initially, you feel a bit dizzy. If this happens, stop, breathe normally and when it passes, you may resume.

Many people have put off meditation because they believe that it is difficult to achieve. Being still is one thing, but trying to stop one thought from jumping to another is something else. Like all good things in life, it requires effort and won't happen overnight. It may be tricky at first, but it is achievable. Like any other skill, it requires commitment and practice. Start with a few minutes and slowly build up to what suits you. Regularly praising this will build your ability to meditate with ease. Once you have achieved the ability to meditate successfully and start to reap the rewards, there is no turning back. Not only will you achieve clearer insight, but you will deal with stressful situations better.

Quieting the mind is a skill that requires keeping thoughts out of your awareness and focus. Empaths new to meditation and who struggle initially should realize that it will often fail in early attempts, but they should not give up in frustration. As a beginner, one needs to acknowledge that one may not be able to calm one's mind for twenty minutes on a first try. It may take weeks, months or even longer to be successful at this. Empaths have to train their brains to do what it has never done before, that is to keep thoughts and feelings out. No matter how frustrating the first day is, remain committed to a few minutes every day. The strength and relief that empaths can achieve from this technique are bountiful. It is a method that will continue to reward you in many ways.

Chapter Nine: How Empaths Have Helped the World

Empaths have succeeded and made an impact on today's world by embracing their unique qualities. Their ability to identify and step into another person's shoes has allowed empaths all over the world, and through the course of history, to make a social impact and inspire others.

Empaths in Politics

Barack Obama has made numerous speeches referencing the "*empathy deficit*" as modern day society's biggest issue. He believes that by developing a culture of empathy, we can solve many of the issues we face today across the world. He preaches understanding and empathy rather than hatred and division. One of his famous quotes is: *"Learning to stand in somebody else's shoes, to see through their eyes, that's how peace begins. And it's up to you to make that happen."*

Way back in 1971, C.P. Ellis, demonstrated his empathic ability. He found himself at a top position in the Ku Klux Klan. He initially joined, following in the footsteps of his father, because he believed that all black people were the cause of the poverty his family was facing. He was part of a community forum to solve racial tensions in schools. He headed this forum with a woman he hated. She was a black activist named Ann Atwater. However, this provided a platform for him to identify with her needs and realized that they were fighting the same cause and he was blaming black people instead of the real culprits who were white capitalists and politicians. He later became a civil rights campaigner and he and Ann remained friends. He publicly denounced his Ku Klux Klan membership and was able to take responsibility for his choices by fighting for rights of all people including black people in America through his ability to empathize.

We cannot mention politics and empaths by mentioning the famous Mahatma Gandhi. In his crusade for Indian independence from British rule, he decided to undergo an empathic immersion. He believed that he could not truly fight for the rights of people until he fully understood them. He substituted his barrister's suit for a loincloth. He lived the life of the peasant farmers of India from 1917 to 1930. He embraced all aspects of their lives even the jobs that were considered 'untouchable' to many, like cleaning latrines. He penetrated deep racial divides in India and uttered words which are still relevant today: *"I am a Muslim! And a Hindu and a Christian and a Jew—and so are all of you."* This is a statement that embodies all that it is to be an empath.

Empathic Actors

Effective actors need to fully embrace the roles they undertake. For this, they have to find ways to deeply identify and understand their characters. Many dedicated actors have undergone empathy immersion in order to fully understand the characters they intend to play. Hillary Swank won an Oscar for her role as a transgendered man, Brandon Teena. His male friends raped and him when they discovered that he had female genitalia. Hillary Swank also undertook an empathy immersion for the preparation of this role by cutting off her hair and dressing in her husband's clothes for a month. In this way, she identified with people with a sexual identity crisis and the harassment they face. Through her role, she raised awareness and tried to bring about understanding and empathy for gay, lesbian, and transgender people.

Charlize Theron gained weight for her roles as an overworked mother of three children and her role as a serial killer. She did this so that she could fully feel what life was like for these characters. This ability to embrace an immersive empathy makes her successful at acting and raises empathy in the audience.

Empathy Through Authors

George Orwell immersed himself into an empathic experience to discover what life was really like for every day working class people. He lived as a beggar on the streets of London as a means to understand oppressed people. He raised awareness through his book 'Down and Out in Paris and London' and continued to highlight marginalized communities.

Harriet Beecher Stowe fought against slavery in 1852 through her book titled 'Uncle Tom's Cabin'. She highlighted the horrors that slaves went through, which eventually led to rebellions and the American Civil War.

Social Activists

In 1206, Giovanni Bernadone, better known as *St. Francis of Assisi* identified with the poor by being a beggar for a day. This experience led him to serve the poor and lepers in Rome.

Many years later, in 1959, a white Texas-born man decided to see what life was like as a black individual living in America by dyeing his skin black. He wrote a book to describe his experiences called 'Black Like Me'. He outlined in his book how people need to use empathy to change their biases and stereotypes and treat people better. His message in his book states: *"If only we could put ourselves in the shoes of others to see how we would react, then we might become aware of the injustices of discrimination and the tragic inhumanity of every kind of prejudice."*

Conclusion

We hope that in reading this book you have gained insight and understanding of what it is to be an empath. We hope that this understanding brings peace, acceptance, and clarity into your life. We hope that the tools, techniques, and ways provided will help empaths cope with the world. It may be a difficult journey of discovery for an empath, but there will be much to be grateful for. Using the strengths of an empath like intuition, compassion, depth, and a connection to people and the surrounding gives an empath the capacity to help others. In a world that lacks compassion and kindness, empaths are more needed than ever. Empaths from all over the world and across different eras have helped to champion social justice, causes, or raise awareness of the plight of others in some way. Empowered empaths are what the world needs now.

There is much for an empath to be grateful for. Empaths can experience the greatest joys and passion, are synchronized to the beauty and energy of the world, can show compassion, awareness, and great depth. These gifts must shine into the world, enlightening it and bringing healing for everyone. For this to happen, empaths must listen to their intuition, instincts, and feelings. They must strengthen their ability to remain centered when surrounded by chaos and negativity. Empaths must embrace who they are and accept their sensitivities. When this happens, they can enhance the lives of the people around them. When empaths do not learn how to cope with and recognize the feeling of being overwhelmed or being stressed, it can lead to depression, panic attacks, addiction, food, medication, and isolation.

The strategies of setting boundaries, time limits, and shielding techniques can help empaths navigate a sea of negative energies. Together with meditation, time apart, and being in nature, empaths can empower themselves and remain centered and grounded majority of the time. These are all strategies that can be learned and mastered with practice.

When empaths are surrounded by love and peace, they will blossom and offer the world many gifts. When they are surrounded by negativity, pain, and loss, they will absorb all these emotions and result in feeling exhausted, overwhelmed, and drained. An empath's sensitivity can lead them to shy away from intimate relationships, but empaths can enjoy the comforts and joys of intimacy and cohabitation. By regularly practicing the techniques in this book, empaths will be armed with survival and coping strategies with which to negotiate the modern world.

Empaths can feel and be open instead of choosing isolation and numbness. Empaths can surrender and feel instead of constantly blocking. With the acceptance and understanding of what it is to be an empath, empaths can communicate and educate family and friends, thereby, fostering a deeper understanding and connection between them. When supported by people who appreciate and honor an empath's abilities, empaths can grow and blossom. The purpose of empaths is to use their sensitivities and compassion to show and create love in the world.

www.ingramcontent.com/pod-product-compliance
Lightning Source LLC
Chambersburg PA
CBHW071456080526
44587CB00014B/2120